The Library of the Middle Ages™

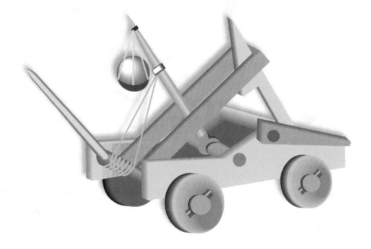

Islamic Weapons, Warfare, and Armies

Muslim Military Operations Against the Crusaders

Paul Hilliam

The Rosen Publishing Group, Inc., New York

This late fifteenth-century Turkish painting depicts two warriors in combat.

The Early Spread of Islam

any non-Muslims believe that Muhammad (AD 570–632) was the founder of Islam. Muslims, followers of the religion of Islam, on the other hand, believe that Allah, their god, has always existed, so it follows that Islam has always existed. Muhammad is seen as the final prophet. Nevertheless, dating from his lifetime, the religion of Islam started a dramatic period of expansion.

During the seventh and eighth centuries, Islam spread throughout the Middle East and then across North Africa and into Spain in the west. In the east it reached as far as India. This book tells the story of the weapons and armor used by Muslim soldiers during the Middle Ages, along with details about the organization and tactics of Islamic armies.

Muslim historians have left accurate contemporary accounts of the various wars that occurred during this turbulent period, so we have been able to include descriptions of some of these dramatic events in this book. In addition, we will learn that although much of the Middle Ages was characterized by violent battles, many Muslim rulers were

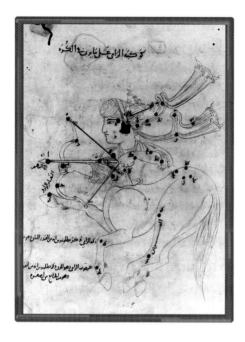

Two drawings of constellations from the *Book of Fixed Stars* by the Arab astronomer Abd al-Rahman bin Umar al-Sufi (AD 903–986). Much of our early astronomical knowledge, including the names of many stars, comes from the Arabs, who were more advanced in the sciences than the Europeans at this time.

(migration) is regarded as the start of the Islamic calendar.

During the following years, Muhammad engaged in a series of attacks on the people of Makkah. At first only trading caravans were ambushed, but tension between the two towns quickly escalated. The first battle fought in the name of Islam was at Badr in 624, when Muhammad with a band of three hundred followers beat a much larger force. This was taken by some as a divine sign. However, there were setbacks, and in 625 at Uhud, just outside Medina, the Muslims were defeated and Muhammad himself was injured. Finally, as support grew for the Prophet, a treaty paved the way for Muhammad to return to Makkah.

Tradition relates that Muhammad rode into Makkah on a white camel at the head of an army of ten thousand, declaring "Truth is come. Falsehood has fled away!" Acting with great insight, Muhammad won the loyalty of his leading opponents by offering them positions of authority. The idols at the Kaaba were smashed and the building was dedicated to the worship of Allah. Ever since, Muslims have faced the Kaaba in prayer five times each day. At least once in a lifetime Muslims are expected to undertake a *hajj* (pilgrimage) to the holy city.

Muhammad died in 632. By that time much of Arabia had converted to the new religion, but it was during the two hundred years after his death that Islam was to see its most rapid expansion.

Jihad

Muslims believe that they have a religious duty to establish and promote life "in the way of Allah." The term *jihad* means "struggle" or "exertion," and there are two types of jihad. The "greater jihad" means the struggle against the sort of evil all people face in their everyday lives. The "lesser jihad" refers to legal or religiously sanctioned war.

In the early years following the death of Muhammad, Muslim laws of war were based upon the teachings of the Koran, and Muslim armies spread Islam through conquest, treaties, and conversions. Abu Bakr, the first caliph, or successor to Muhammad, laid down more exact rules for warfare. War was only to be declared once a general call to convert to Islam had been issued and ignored. Muslim troops were forbidden to kill children, women, and old men. Trees and crops and farm animals were not to be destroyed, but they could be used for food. One Islamic general went further, ordering that civilians and especially farmers be treated with respect. Much later, in 1167, a legal scholar named Ibn Rushd wrote a further treatise in response to the European invasions during the Crusades. He claimed that jihad was essentially defensive.

Some people welcomed Islamic rule, especially where it replaced a less tolerant authority. Christians and Jews were regarded as *ahl al-kitab* or "people of the book [the Bible]." Their religious buildings were protected and they were allowed to continue worshiping as before. All conquered peoples were expected to pay taxes, but they paid a lower rate if they converted to Islam. Not surprisingly, many converted.

The Early Spread of Islam Under the Caliphs

Muhammad died without nominating a successor and so a caliph was elected. The word caliph means "successor," and the caliph fulfilled the role of political and religious leader, as well as being "commander of the faithful," effectively a general. The first four caliphs were known as "rightly guided," because they had known Muhammad personally and during this time Islam won important battles against the Byzantines and Sassanians. They also took Egypt, much of North Africa, and Palestine, with its capital, Jerusalem.

The third caliph, Uthman, was assassinated, and Ali, who was Muhammad's son-in-law and cousin, was elected as the fourth caliph. However, Ali's election was disputed by the influential Umayya family, who claimed that Ali's supporters had been involved in Uthman's death. As a result of this dispute, a major split occurred within Islam, from which two Muslim groups emerged.

The Saracens assault the city of Messina in Sicily around AD 875, from a fourteenth-century Byzantine manuscript illustration. The concept of jihad, or holy war, meant that the Islamic faith could be spread through war and conquest.

The Shiite Muslims maintained that the caliph should be a descendant of Muhammad, while the Sunni Muslims believed that the caliph should be elected. Having removed Ali, the Sunni Muslims elected Mu'awiya as the first Umayyad caliph. Later, a descendant of Muhammad, Abbas, became caliph after a rebellion, and the Abbasids came to power. The Umayyad dynasty (661–750) ruled like kings, in great splendor from a palace in Damascus, while

The imposing thirteenth-century Arab fortress of Qalaat Najim in the Euphrates Valley of modern Syria

the later Abbasid dynasty (749–1258) moved its power base to Baghdad. After the Umayyad and Abbasid periods, control of the Islamic world became less centralized as groups such as the Fatimids in Egypt and the Seljuk Turks increased their power.

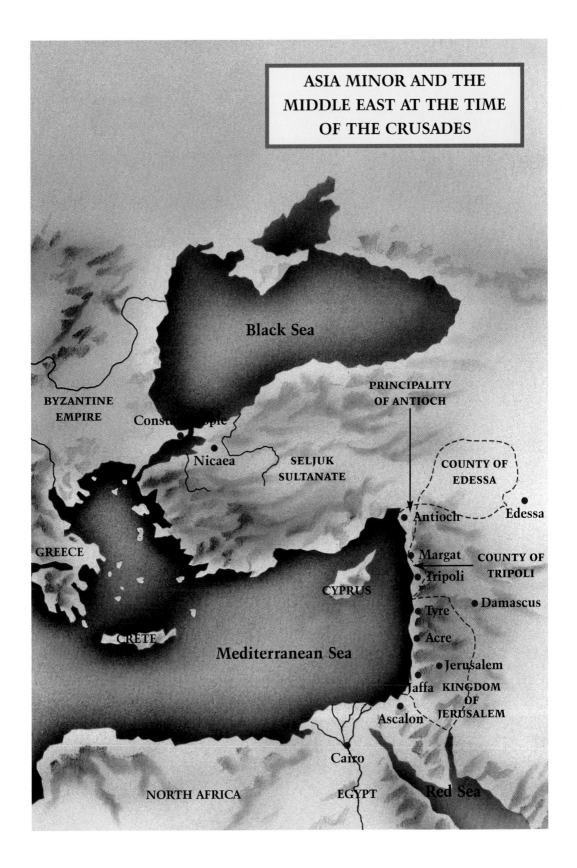

ASIA MINOR AND THE
MIDDLE EAST AT THE TIME
OF THE CRUSADES

Black Sea

PRINCIPALITY
OF ANTIOCH

BYZANTINE
EMPIRE   Constantinople

Nicaea   SELJUK
                SULTANATE

                                COUNTY OF
                                  EDESSA

                            Antioch   Edessa

GREECE   Margat   COUNTY OF
                                Tripoli   TRIPOLI

                    CYPRUS   Damascus
                                Tyre

                                Acre
CRETE
            Mediterranean Sea   Jerusalem

                                Jaffa   KINGDOM
                                          OF
                                Ascalon JERUSALEM

                    Cairo

NORTH AFRICA   EGYPT   Red Sea

The siege of Baghdad by the Mongols, who invaded Muslim lands in the thirteenth century. The expansion of the Mongols drove the nomadic Seljuk Turks of central Asia to the west, where they founded the Ottoman Empire in what is modern Turkey.

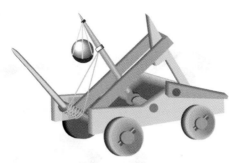

Islamic Weapons and Armor

The early contact that Muslim armies had with the Byzantine and Sassanian Empires influenced the development of Islamic weapons and armor. The Sassanian Empire was particularly rich with the iron ore needed for the manufacture of weapons, so controlling this area became important for the Islamic arms trade.

Weapons for Hand-to-Hand Combat

The prophet Muhammad said, "Swords are the keys to Paradise. He who draws the sword in the path of God has sworn allegiance to God." Other weapons used in hand-to-hand combat included daggers, single-edged and double-edged axes, the mace (a metal club), and the ball and chain. But the sword was always the most highly prized weapon.

Most early Muslim swords were straight and double-edged, with a relatively small quillion, or cross guard, and pommel (the bulb or nut-shaped end that prevents the hand from losing its grip on the handle).

A fifteenth-century gold-plated Persian ceremonial dagger with a double-edged blade. It bears an inscription that reads: "May all your affairs be according to your wishes; may the Lord be your guardian."

From about the end of the thirteenth century, the slightly curved, single-edged sword started to appear. This is usually referred to as a saber, and it had a slight thickening of the blade toward the tip. From the fifteenth century on, highly curved, almost crescent-shaped, single-edged swords were increasingly used. These scimitars had their origin in the Far East. They were light, with extremely sharp steel blades, and they could be used by soldiers while on horseback to slash at the enemy. It was common to carry two such swords.

Swordsmiths in Damascus in the Middle East and in Toledo in Muslim Spain were held in high regard. The handles on most expensive ceremonial swords were covered with gems, and the blades were decorated with patterns made from valuable metals.

Longbows and Crossbows

Archery was a highly respected skill, during times of both war and peace. Muhammad himself was a fine archer and commented that "The angels attend no human sport except archery." Many Muslims regarded archery practice almost as

A bronze mace head from twelfth-century Persia. It has six radiating flanges, or ribs. The mace was a short club with a heavy head, like this one, at the end, and it was swung like an axe or hammer.

a religious obligation, and games were frequently held. Shooting over a long distance was popular and distances of up to half a mile were recorded. Archers developed accuracy by shooting at targets, but the ultimate test was to hit an object, perhaps a fruit such as a gourd suspended from a pole, while passing by at high speeds on horseback.

Bows made of solid wood were common, but the composite bow was better. Wood, imported sometimes from India or Africa, was shaped and then glued on either side of a layer of horn, while sinew (animal gut or tendon) would be attached to the outside of the bow facing the target. While the horn compressed, the sinew stretched to give the bow extra power. The overall length of the composite bow was not long, so it could be handled easily while riding. Although it was rarely able to penetrate the sort of plate armor worn by European knights in the later Middle Ages, its construction and curved design at each end meant that it was a very powerful bow for its length.

Members of the Muslim light cavalry were usually equipped with bows and arrows held in a quiver and maybe

falconry, archery, and fencing. There are also sections devoted to fire-throwing weapons. Contemporary pictures also show soldiers holding grenades and rockets, with clearly visible fuses and detonators. To strike terror into the enemy, it was said that some Muslim troops would cover themselves with a sticky fireproof substance, then mount fireworks on themselves before raiding an enemy camp at night.

Armor and Other Clothing

Throughout the Middle Ages, Muslim soldiers preferred light armor that allowed them to move as freely as possible, especially while fighting on horseback. A short chain-mail coat was the most common form of protection. Sometimes horses were also given chain-mail coats. Leather armor, boiled in paraffin and wax and then covered with rectangular metal plates, was also popular, modeled after the armor worn by the Mongols of central Asia who invaded the Muslim lands in the early thirteenth century. It was not unusual to wear loose-fitting robes over armor. Colors for these robes and turbans, or cloth head-coverings, changed from time to time and from place to place according to fashion. Uniforms were not standardized features of Muslim armies, although Umayyad soldiers usually wore white. During the Abbasid period, soldiers were ordered by Caliph al-Saffah to wear black.

The heavy suits of armor made from plate metal that were developed in European countries during the late Middle Ages were not adopted by Muslim troops, mainly because of the extreme heat of the desert. Another garment worn as a result of Mongol influence was a lightweight but densely

A steel sword from twelfth-century Persia. Its blade is straight and single-edged. After the thirteenth century, slightly curved swords, called sabers, started to appear.

woven silk undershirt. If an arrow pierced the outer chain mail it would force the silk fibers into the flesh, which would help plug the wound. The arrow could then be removed by pulling gently at the silk shirt.

Helmets, called tombacs, were conical and could be worn with a turban curled around the outside, possibly to deflect the sun's rays. A chain-mail coif or neck guard was usually attached to the bottom rim, and some helmets had a short spike on top. Illustrations show that plumes were also popular. Shields gave further protection. They were made either of metal or leather mounted on a wooden frame and were usually circular and relatively small.

Castles and Sieges

A Muslim army on campaign fortified its camp by surrounding it with a circle of ditches. When an area had been conquered, any captured fort or castle would be occupied, rebuilt, and strengthened. In this way the Muslims were quick to adopt a range of architectural defenses. They were influenced in particular by Byzantine models.

During the Crusades, both the Arabs and Europeans copied and adapted the techniques of castle defense and siege warfare used by the opposing army. Krak des Chevaliers, for example, was a Muslim castle to which the crusaders added outer concentric walls. Muslim armies, for their part, used European designs for siege machines, including the *burj*, a wooden tower; the *dubb ba*, a battering ram under a wooden shed; and the *manjanq*, a stone-throwing catapult. The Muslims were experts at digging mines to bring down castle walls, and of course they used fire-bombs to destroy enemy siege machines.

A sixteenth-century Turkish chain-mail and plate-armor coat. The helmet is turban-shaped and features a skirt of chain-mail armor.

Arab cities, such as Baghdad, were given impressive defensive walls. Some early mosques, such as the Great Mosque at Kairouan in Tunisia, look more like forts. All over the Islamic world, watchtowers were built in order for guards to keep watch and give warning of enemy troop movements. In the end, though, it was the invention of the cannon that ended this great period of fort and castle building.

The siege of Damascus in 1148 by the soldiers of the Second Crusade, from a fifteenth-century French manuscript illumination

Going to War

In the early days of Islam, Muslim forces were small and disorganized. They carried out raids on neighboring towns and trading caravans, fighting to spread the faith. Slaves would go to war alongside their masters, often for the promise of freedom but sometimes under threat of punishment if they did not fight. Both slaves and their owners believed they would be rewarded in paradise (heaven) if they died in battle.

The promise of booty following conquest was also important, giving all who fought the prospect of wealth. According to a reported saying of the Prophet, Muhammad put Amr ibn al-As in charge of troops before his conquest of Egypt with the words "May God keep you safe and bring you much booty." The general replied, "I did not become a Muslim for the sake of wealth, but for the sake of submission to God." The Prophet responded, "Honest wealth is good for an honest man." In later centuries, rules were drawn up to govern the division of booty, so that, for example, one captured camel was worth ten sheep and a cavalryman received twice the booty given to a foot soldier because he had a horse to maintain.

also aimed at moving targets such as stuffed animals mounted on carts rolled down hillsides. Wrestling, hunting, polo, mathematics, reading, and even gentlemanly conduct might have been in the curriculum. Young recruits were given opportunities to carry out border raids in enemy countries. Slaves who successfully finished their training might be given their freedom. Commanders gained experience organizing large numbers of troops by drilling soldiers on parade or during military reviews.

Spies and Intelligence

The use of spies to gather intelligence about an enemy was crucial before going to war. Muslim rulers were keen to tap into whatever sources were available. Spies were sent abroad but were also employed at home to keep an eye on suspect military commanders. They were well paid and their families were looked after and protected when they were away from home. Ambassadors and people on official missions and merchants visiting neighboring countries were questioned closely when they returned. During the Middle Ages, Muslims generally showed little interest in the military activities of European countries. Their inhabitants were regarded as brave and strong but were also believed to be rather ignorant and dirty.

Preventing information from reaching the enemy was equally important, so merchants visiting from other countries were required to stay in designated lodges where they could be kept under surveillance in case they were reporting back to an enemy. Troop commanders might be given their

The formidable approach to the Citadel, a mountaintop fortress in Aleppo, Syria. The Muslims and the Europeans copied castle- and fortress-building techniques from each other.

orders just before departure on a mission to prevent their movements being leaked.

Messengers accompanied by guards on horseback used an organized network of stations where they could pick up fresh horses, while lines of hilltop beacons were lit to send prearranged signals. In addition, it was the Arabs who first developed the use of carrier pigeons in order to send information. There are stories of birds being captured en route and

Another view of the southern approach to the Citadel in Aleppo, Syria. Steeply sloping walls and protruding towers that allowed defenders to fire into the flanks of attackers were common features of both Christian and Muslim fortresses.

being sent off again carrying false information! Other stories suggest that pigeons, rather than carrying written messages, were covered in different scents and that these were used as codes! Meanwhile, the crusaders trained hawks to bring down carrier pigeons, particularly when they were besieging Muslim castles.

Propaganda, or the spreading of false information to the enemy, was an important psychological weapon. A fourteenth-century Turkish ruler terrified some Romanian prisoners by leading them to think that his men were cannibals. He then released them so that they spread panic when they returned home!

Transport

The camel featured in the local raids led by Muhammad and his early followers, but as a result of their conflicts with the Byzantine and Sassanian Empires, the Arabs adopted wider use of the horse. There were several breeds including the African barb, the Turcoman, or "golden horse," and the smaller but tough central Asian horse. However, the Arabian horse was renowned as the most intelligent. Government-controlled stables engaged in selective breeding, although the nomadic bedouin tribes who lived in the desert were reputed to produce the finest horses. By the seventh century, the Arabs were using metal stirrups and wooden-framed saddles.

The European knights who journeyed to the Middle East during the Crusades are usually imagined to have used larger, heavier horses that could bear the weight of men in full armor. In reality, this sort of heavy armor was worn a little later. For much of the period of the Crusades, there was probably little difference in the size of the horses of the opposing armies, although the Arabian horse was faster and had more endurance and agility. One problem the crusaders did face was maintaining a steady supply of horses and fodder, whereas Arab horses were usually put out to graze.

A European depiction of the capture of the city of Acre in AD 1191 during the Third Crusade. This crusade was led by King Richard of England and King Philip of France.

When on the move, mules, donkeys, and camels were used to transport equipment, allowing horses to remain rested and ready for battle. In the deserts of North Africa and the Middle East, the single-humped Arabian camel, or dromedary, was faster than a horse and able to cope with the hot, dry climate, while farther north and east the two-humped Bactrian camel could endure colder weather and rougher terrain.

One notable feature of Arab armies was their speed of movement. It was possible for a small group of mounted troops to cover about fifty miles a day. In contrast, a typical European army would cover about twenty miles a day because most of its troops would be on foot, accompanied by supply wagons. The famous Muslim commander Saladin (1137–1193) trained his armies to move faster and remain on campaign for longer periods of time. In addition to supply trains, traveling markets were encouraged, giving locals the opportunity to sell produce to troops.

Movement of troops and horses by sea was made possible by specially designed galleys called tarda. These were designed so that they could be beached at the stern for disembarkation. Landing troops on a foreign coast gave the advantage of surprise, as it was more difficult for an enemy to judge when or where a landing might take place. Some ships were armed with stone-throwing catapults called mangonels. Other ships might be equipped with tall wooden siege towers that were protected by animal hides from being set on fire. These gave soldiers the chance to climb into coastal forts and onto port defenses. Fire ships were another way to attack a port, so defensive chains were stretched over harbor entrances to prevent such ships from reaching the town.

A portrait of the Kurdish general Saladin. He became vizier of Egypt in AD 1169, united the Muslims of Egypt and Syria, and drove the crusaders out of most of the Holy Land.

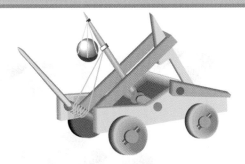

Wars in the Middle East and the Balkans

I n AD 638, the city of Jerusalem surrendered to Caliph Umar. Although this was a holy city for both Jews and Christians, it was also a holy city for Muslims and therefore one they wanted to control. The importance of Jerusalem for Muslims is evident in the story of the Night Journey, which claims that one night Muhammad flew from Mecca to Jerusalem on a *buraq*, or winged horse. In Jerusalem, Muhammad is said to have landed on the remains of the Jewish Temple of Solomon. From there he ascended to heaven where he met the former prophets of Judaism and Christianity. He was then acknowledged as the final prophet and was told by God the times of daily prayer all Muslims were to observe.

In 692, the Dome of the Rock was completed, built over the site in Jerusalem where Muhammad landed and ascended into heaven. From this point Jerusalem became a focal point of Islamic pilgrimage, second only to Mecca and Medina. The Muslims who occupied the city treated the Jews and Christians well, although non-Muslims were expected to pay a *jizyah*, or tax, in order to enjoy freedom

A European view of Saladin's army, from a fourteenth-century French manuscript

of worship. Christian pilgrims making the long and difficult journey from Europe were sometimes charged a "safety tax" as they traveled through Muslim-held lands, but they were generally tolerated. So the Church of the Holy Sepulchre, built over the site of Jesus' crucifixion, continued to receive visitors.

Two events brought about the call for a Christian crusade against the Muslims in the Middle East. In 1009, al-Hakim, the caliph of Egypt, destroyed the Church of the Holy Sepulchre and started to persecute Jews and Christians. Then in 1071, the Seljuk Turks inflicted a huge defeat upon the

Byzantine army at Manzikert and followed that by capturing Jerusalem from their fellow Muslims. They were more warlike and lacking in the tolerance extended by earlier Arab Muslim rulers in the area. Alexius I, the Byzantine emperor, appealed directly to Pope Urban II for help, fearing the Seljuk forces would soon attack Constantinople.

In 1095, the pope spoke at a council of church leaders at Clermont in France. He called for nobles and knights in Europe to recapture the Holy Land, saying, "Christ himself will be your leader. Wear his cross as your badge. If you are killed your sins will be pardoned." As a result, during the next two centuries, various armies set off for Palestine, and soldiers cut cross-shaped cloths to sew on their tunics. The Latin word *crux*, meaning "cross," gave rise to the word "crusade."

The First Crusade did indeed capture Jerusalem in 1099, and there followed a considerable slaughter of Jewish and Muslim civilians. Seljuk power was waning due to internal political struggles, and the Muslims faced more threatening invasions from the Mongols in the east. Soon the crusaders established four independent states on the coast of the Mediterranean, collectively knows as Outremer, meaning the "land over the water." However, by 1187, Jerusalem had been recaptured by Salah-ed-Din, better known as Saladin.

The short period of Christian domination in the area ended when Saladin, the ruler of Egypt, swept up into Palestine. By laying siege to Tiberias on the shores of Lake Galilee, he managed to draw the Christian forces out of Jerusalem. Exhausted after their march and short of water, the crusaders camped on a hill with two peaks, known as the Horns of Hattin. When they

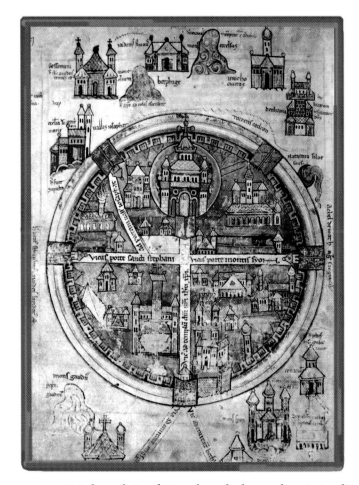

A twelfth-century map of Jerusalem, which was captured by the crusaders in AD 1099 and recaptured by the armies of Saladin in 1187.

awoke in the morning, their camp had been surrounded by bonfires which gave off thick smoke, causing confusion and disorientation. The Muslim cavalry completely destroyed the army of Guy, king of Jerusalem, and took hold of his city. Saladin's greatest opponent during the Third Crusade was Richard I of England, but the Muslims held on to Jerusalem despite memorable victories won by each side.

Muslim strategy during the Crusades was to surprise and outmaneuver the enemy, and avoid at all costs the charge of knights armed with lances. Richard I had led such an assault with devastating success at the Battle of Arsuf. Whenever it was possible to reduce an enemy on the march by ambush, the speed of the Arab horses gave Muslim soldiers the advantage. But if open battle proved unavoidable, then their infantry would be placed behind

A Turkish bombard, cast for Sultan Mehmed II in 1464. It was made of bronze and weighed twenty tons. The cannonballs weighed over 600 pounds each. The sultan used cannons like this one to breach the walls of Constantinople, which he captured in 1453.

soft sand or rocky ground to slow down the knights' horses. At the same time they would try to ensure that the sun was behind them, or that enemies charged into a head wind that would blow dust into their eyes. Meanwhile, Muslim archers on horseback would ride as close as possible, showering knights with arrows and shooting their horses beneath them.

None of the later Crusades achieved lasting European dominance in the Middle East, and overall the Muslim world regarded the Crusades as relatively insignificant. For their part, the Europeans benefited a great deal from their contact with the Arab world. They admired and copied the design of Muslim castles, learned new skills in mathematics such as the use of Arabic numerals, and took exotic spices and silks back home.

The Ottoman Empire

The Seljuk Empire finally collapsed under the continued Mongol invasions from central Asia. Nomads, fleeing west for safety, established towns in Anatolia (modern-day Turkey), each under the control of a local ruler. The descendants of one such ruler, Osman, who ruled from 1300 to 1326, established the Osmanli Empire, better known as the Ottoman Empire.

Osman's son Orhan started the Muslim invasion of Europe. By 1372, the king of Bulgaria had been forced into submission, and soon most of the Balkan rulers were obliged to pay an annual tax to the Ottoman sultan and to help protect the empire's borders. Uprisings were crushed by Bayezid, the fourth sultan, who was nicknamed the Thunderbolt. Then a European army, sent to halt further Muslim expansion, was crushed in 1396 at the Battle of Nicopolis. A combined force of knights from several countries charged hopelessly at Bayezid's army of 60,000 men. Ten thousand prisoners were decapitated after the battle.

Of the many battles during the time of the Ottomans, two are particularly worth noting: the siege of Constantinople in 1453 and the Battle of Lepanto in 1571, the first a victory for the Ottomans and the second a defeat. It was Mehmed II, "the Conqueror," who ruled from 1451 to 1481, who laid siege to and finally captured Constantinople. Thanks to the design and strength of its triple walls, the city withstood Muslim attacks for seven centuries. But now Muslim forces had use of cannons, modeled after those developed in Europe.

The strategic importance of Constantinople was huge, as it guarded the narrow entrance to the Black Sea. It was also of symbolic significance as it had been the eastern capital of the former Roman Empire and thereafter the capital of the Byzantine Empire. As the Ottomans advanced toward the city, scholars fled to Europe and in particular Italy, taking with them knowledge long forgotten in western Europe since the time of the ancient Greeks. The rebirth of learning in Europe, known as the Renaissance, was fueled by the Islamic attack in the east and helped to bring about the end of the Middle Ages.

The ten thousand defenders of Constantinople were surrounded by Ottoman forces numbering over one hundred thousand troops. Their escape route by sea was also cut off by a Muslim blockade. On May 22, 1453, it was said that an eclipse of the moon created the spectacle of a crescent shape—the symbol of Islam—in the night sky above the Muslim camp. Not surprisingly, the Christian troops in the city took this as a bad omen. In the early hours of May 29, the walls of Constantinople were breached by cannon fire, but this first attack was repulsed. Trumpets were blown in an effort to distract the defenders before a second unsuccessful attack was launched. One account of the siege suggests that the Byzantine Christians had accidentally left open one of the city's seaports and that elite Turkish troops stormed this gate in overwhelming numbers.

Constantinople had fallen. The domed church Hagia Sophia was converted into a mosque and the city was renamed Istanbul. It served as the capital of an Ottoman Empire that was to last for another four hundred years. Under Sulayman the Magnificent, the Ottomans continued to expand into

A siege tower, from a fifteenth-century manuscript illumination

Europe, and in 1529 they reached almost as far as Vienna, the Austrian capital. It was not until 1571 that they suffered their first major defeat at the sea Battle of Lepanto.

The siege of Constantinople had shown the Ottomans that they needed to build and maintain a large naval fleet. In 1565, a fleet of 181 ships attacked Malta, the base of the Knights of St. John, the final remnant of an earlier crusading force. The knights repelled the attack, but this episode convinced the Europeans that the Ottoman naval threat had to be dealt with.

Pope Pius V formed a Holy League, consisting of naval forces from Italy and Spain. Three hundred galleys under the command of Don Juan of Spain met the Ottoman fleet off the coast of Greece on September 17, 1571. Splitting his ships into three groups, Don Juan advanced toward the crescent-shaped enemy line. Light cannons on the bows were fired and the infantry used muskets. As the two fleets collided, boats interlocked and there was furious hand-to-hand fighting during which the Ottoman commander, Ali Pasha, was captured and immediately beheaded. After four hours of fighting, the papal forces had lost eight thousand men, compared to Turkish losses of twenty-five thousand. After the battle, twelve thousand Turkish galley slaves were released as the Holy League celebrated its victory.

One Spaniard injured at Lepanto was Miguel de Cervantes, who later wrote the classic novel *Don Quixote,* which is about the exploits of an old knight. It is also interesting to note that a life-size replica of Don Juan's galley can be seen in Barcelona's medieval Royal Shipyard. Life onboard such a galley, whether Spanish or Ottoman, was so appalling that a ship could be smelled before it could be seen coming over the horizon!

Although the Ottoman fleet was rebuilt within three years, the Battle of Lepanto was an important victory for the Christian forces. They had shown that the Muslim advance on Europe could be contained.

The siege of Constantinople in 1453 by the Turks, from a sixteenth-century Italian fresco, an image painted into wet limestone on a church wall. The city became the capital of the Ottoman Empire, which lasted for another 400 years.

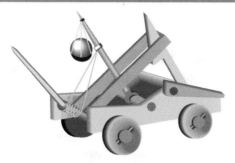

The Moors in Spain and the Mughals in India

I n AD 711, a Muslim army crossed the narrow Strait of Gibraltar and invaded Spain. This army consisted of Berbers and Arabs from North Africa known as Moors. One account of the invasion claims that their leader, Tariq, spread fear among the locals when he landed by commanding his ships to be destroyed, signaling to all that he was serious in his intent to conquer. The Moors quickly rustled horses from neighboring farms and easily overcame the hastily assembled army of Roderick, the last king of the Visigoths.

Originally from eastern Europe, the Visigoths were themselves invaders in Spain, but the people of the Iberian Peninsula included many Jews as well as Christians, and they preferred the more tolerant attitudes of their new Muslim rulers. Within a decade most of Spain was under Muslim control, apart from Asturias and the Basque region in the far north, which remained Christian kingdoms. The Moors called their new province al-Andalus. Looking at a map, one can see that Andalusia is still a region of southern Spain.

The Mongols, from whom the Mughals were descended, originated as nomads from the steppes (or grassy planes) of central Asia, where they lived in large villages of tents, while tending flocks of animals. Under Genghis Khan, "Conqueror of the World" (who reigned from 1160 to 1227), they had taken control of a vast area stretching from China in the east to the Black Sea in the west. What made the Mongols so feared was their ability to surprise an enemy by covering huge distances on horseback at great speed. Each warrior took with him a string of fresh horses, which would graze freely when the army stopped. An army of ten thousand Mongols might have over a hundred thousand horses with them.

In 1258, the Mongols captured the Muslim city of Baghdad, where, according to contemporary historians, they slaughtered over eighty thousand people. Moving farther west, the Mongols accepted the surrender of Antioch, the first city captured by the crusaders and still in European hands. However, in 1260, near Nazareth, the Mongols faced a highly disciplined Mamluk army. Lured into an ambush by a feigned retreat, the Mongols were defeated and the heartland of the Islamic world was saved.

The Mongols settled on the eastern borders of the Muslim-held lands and from here turned their attention toward India. In 1398, Timur led a Mongol army into India, where he devastated Delhi. But it was Babur, a Muslim ruler in Afghanistan and a descendent of Timur and Genghis Khan, who was to establish the Mughal dynasty in India. The term Mughal is simply the Persian word for "Mongol." After four earlier raids, Babur finally defeated Ibrahim Lodi, sultan of Delhi. In 1526 at Panipat, his army of twelve thousand defeated the sultan's army of ninety-six thousand. The Indian war elephants, used like modern tanks by the Hindu troops, were no match for the cannons brought by Babur from the Middle East. The following year Babur defeated the Rajputs.

Babur's son Humayan did not have the character or military skills of his father, but his grandson Akbar was a truly great Mughal emperor. Claiming the throne when only thirteen

Mughal elephant armor from around AD 1600. Normally two men rode an elephant, one to control it and the other to do the actual fighting. In spite of their fearsome size, elephants were ineffective against the invading Mongols, who brought cannons with them.

years old, he spent a lifetime on campaign, almost doubling the area over which he ruled. He was ruthless, and after one battle he built a tower using a mixture of mud and human skulls. Most important, though, Akbar brought peace to his kingdom by extending equality to his Hindu subjects. He even won the support of his rivals by marrying a Hindu princess. His son Jahangir was similarly generous and each year gave to the poor gold and jewels equal to his own weight. The next emperor, Shah Jahan, is best known for ordering the construction of the Taj Mahal as a memorial to his wife, who died in 1631 while giving birth to their fourteenth child. Thousands of workers spent over twenty years inlaying white marble

An eighteenth-century Mughal silk doublet reinforced with chain mail from northern India

with semiprecious stones to cover the building with intricate patterns and inscriptions from the Koran.

Shah Jahan's son, Aurangzeb, secured the throne after murdering his two brothers. He was very unpopular because he showed a total intolerance of Hinduism. By the time of the last emperor, Bahdur Shah II, the British had taken control of India. The days of Mughal rule were at an end.

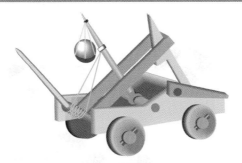

For Further Reading

Bingham, Jane. *Medieval World.* London: Usborne Publishing Ltd, 1999.

Chrisp, Peter. *The Crusades.* Hove, UK: Wayland Publishers, 1992.

Chrisp, Peter. *The Rise of Islam.* Hove, UK: Wayland Publishers, 1991.

Cootes, Richard John. *The Middle Ages.* New York: Longman, 1996.

Ganeri, Anita. *India Under the Mughal Empire.* London: Evans Brothers, 1998.

Gravett , Christopher. *Castle.* London: Dorling Kindersley, 1994.

Konstam, Angus. *Historical Atlas of the Crusades.* New York: Checkmark Books, 2002.

Steele, Philip. *The Medieval World.* London: Kingfisher, 2000.

Williams, Brian. *Forts and Castles*. London: Hamlyn, 1995.

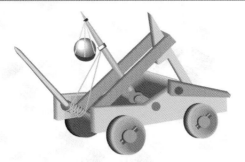

Bibliography

Ellingham, Mark, and John Fisher. *Spain*. London: Rough Guides Ltd., 1992.

Gascoigne, Bamber. *The Great Moghuls*. London: Constable and Company Ltd, 1998.

Jones, John. *The Medieval World*. Walton on Thames, UK: Thomas Nelson Ltd, 1979.

Lunde, Paul. *Islam*. London: Dorling Kindersley, 2002.

Newark, Tim. *The Barbarians*. Poole, UK: Blandford Press, 1985.

Nicolle, David. *Medieval Warfare Source Book*. London: Brockhampton Press, 1998.

Nicolle, David. *The Mongol Warlords*. Poole, UK: Firebird Books Ltd., 1990.

Wilkinson, Frederick. *Arms and Armour*. London: Chancellor Press, 1978.

Index

About the Author

Paul Hilliam is a graduate of London University. He is currently senior master at Derby Grammar School in England, where he enjoys teaching history and religious studies. He has traveled throughout Europe, the Middle East, and India, visiting many sites of historical interest.

Photo Credits

Cover, pp. 32, 38 © The Bridgeman Art Library; p. 4 © Topkapi Museum, Istanbul/Dagli Orti/The Art Archive; p. 8 (top & bottom) © Bodleian Library, Oxford/The Bodleian Library/The Art Archive; p. 11 © Biblioteca Nacional, Madrid/Dagli Orti/The Art Archive; pp. 12, 29, 30 © David Halford; pp. 14, 44 © Sonia Halliday Photographs; pp. 16, 17, 21, 26, 54 © Christie's Images LTD.; pp. 18, 22, 41, 51, 53 © The Board of Trustees of the Armouries; p. 24 © AKG London; p. 36 © British Library, London, UK; p. 40 © Uppsala University Library, Sweden/Dagli Orti/The Art Archive; p. 46 © Moldovita Monastery Romania/Dagli Orti/The Art Archive.

Designer: Geri Fletcher; **Editor:** Jake Goldberg; **Photo Researcher:** Elizabeth Loving